Not a Statistic

Not a Statistic

EMMA WILSON'S STORY OF DETERMINATION THROUGH TRAGEDY

EMMA R. WILSON

CONTENTS

1

HUMBLE BEGINNINGS

My beginnings were humble, as I was the youngest of seven children born to my precious mother, Addie Joyce Robinson, and my father, Fletcher Robinson. I came into the world on December 11, 1966 in the rural town of Banks, Alabama—a rural hamlet nestled in Pike County that is so small there were just 179 residents counted in the 2010 Census.

Mother had her first child at the tender age of thirteen, and I was the last to arrive when she was just twenty. My siblings, from oldest to youngest, are sisters Willa and Minnie, brothers Jimmy, John, and Homer, my sister Dianna—who turned out to be a mentor and model to me—and finally, me. It's interesting, our surnames are slightly different on some of our birth certificates, with some being officially registered as "Robinson's" and others as "Roberson's."

With so many children at such a young age, you might assume that my parents were overwhelmed or had trouble juggling everything. Though our house was bustling, my mother took wonderful care of us, and she was a fastidious housekeeper, while my father worked hard at his job at a local feed mill company. His duties also included maintaining the exterior of our house, yard, and garden, and caring for our hogs. As soon as we children were old enough, our parents had us helping with household chores, outdoor responsibilities, and tending to the animals.

My mother was a most generous and loving soul, and I remember how she loved to have family dinners with all of us gathered around the table. I also recall her coming home from work on Valentine's Day with heart-shaped lollipops for each of us, saying she didn't forget about us and loved us so much. It's these kinds of memories that I'm grateful to have of my mother to this day.

You often hear people who grew up poor talk about how when they were little, they had no idea they wanted for anything, and my siblings and I weren't any different. In many ways, we had everything we needed: a roof over our heads, food, an automobile, and clothing, most of which my mother made because she was a seamstress by trade. Since I was the baby of the family, mine were mostly hand-me-downs from my sister and white families in the area, specifically the Crawleys.

I do remember, however, hearing older people reference our family as being one of Banks' poorest and overhearing conversations between my parents when they discussed not having enough money to cover bills, and needing food, along with other essentials at certain times. It always seemed that we were short of money to cover bills and basic necessities after my father binged for days.

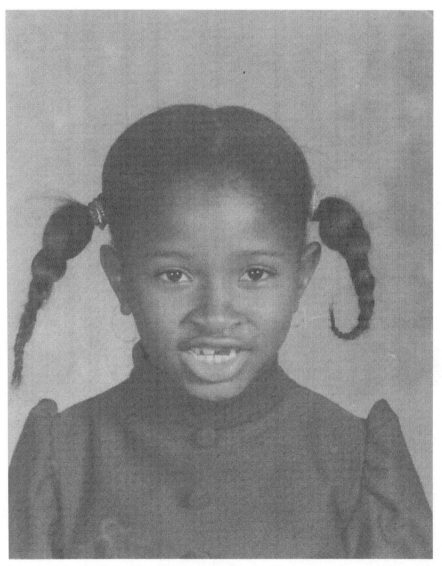

Emma Wilson, photo at Banks Primary School, 1973-1974.

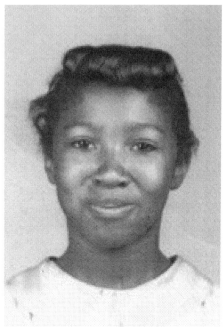

Mother and Robinson Siblings. From left to right back row: Willa, Minnie, Jimmy. Front row:Homer, John, Dianna and Emma.

2

ADDIE BELL PENNINGTON: ALWAYS A ROCK FOR THE FAMILY

My maternal grandmother, Addie Bell Pennington, who always lived next door, consistently helped to fill any deficits we experienced. She was always there for us whenever we were in financial, physical, or emotional need.

When I was a child, my parents and grandmother had houses built on land that they purchased from the Crawleys, a wealthy white family from Banks. They owned the Crawley farm, which consisted of a vast amount of land that was used for field planting (peanuts, cotton, and corn) and cattle and poultry raising. It was also the site where approximately 30 tenant houses were located, all across the acreage.

The tenant houses are where the families lived who worked on the farm. My great-grandmother, grandmother, and parents each lived in one of these homes. The Crawleys sold both my grandmother and parents a plot of land on which to build their homes. In fact, we are fortunate to have in our possession still the deed that reflects the sale of a tract of land by widow Willie T. Crawley and her four siblings to her son Douglas for 100 dollars. This was the tract of land that was eventually sold to my parents. Additionally, we have the deed that reflects the transaction from Douglas Crawley and his wife, Wonnie, "for the sum of one hundred dollars and other good and valuable consideration to us in hand paid by Fletcher Robinson Jr. and Addie P. Robinson." This deed is dated February 3, 1969. The real estate mortgage between my parents and the Farmers Home Administration, United States Department of Agriculture (FHA USDA), reveals that the mortgage was for 8,300 dollars, at 5 ⅛ percent interest, and dated February 4, 1969. Payment in full was expected to be made by February 4, 2002, but the loan was ultimately paid out in full on December 29, 1977, after Mother's death.

The importance of our family members owning their own land and homes, and having these assets over the generations, cannot be underestimated. It allowed us to build wealth that we could pass on to future generations. Since this was withheld from most Black people historically, during and after the Civil War, and even now, my parents were fortunate to have this opportunity. The obstacles to just getting the chance for home and land ownership still plagues the Black community. This predicates the economic inequality that we are still grappling with in this country.

Without being exposed to ownership of a house and land, I wouldn't have been able to dream of owning more.

I speak on the importance of exposure in a later chapter in the book. I know unequivocally that the significance and the possibility of property ownership early on in my life contributed to Rodney and I building our dream to invest in real estate.

My grandmother and her mother, Victoria Baskin, my great-grandmother, worked for most of their lives for the Crawleys, who generations back had owned a plantation that our relatives worked on as enslaved people. The legacy of slavery is peppered with horrific and haunting memories, and my grandmother even talked about seeing a Black man hanging from a tree who had been lynched in her lifetime.

My grandmother picked cotton and peanuts on their land and performed tasks inside their home as well. My uncle also remembers picking cotton on the Crawley family's property as a child, along with all his siblings, including my mother. If there hadn't been this long-standing positive relationship with the Crawleys, it would have been impossible to acquire and purchase land to build homes. As far as I know, my grandmother never worked for anyone throughout her whole life other than the Crawleys. Her lifetime (three generations that I can remember) was spent doing work for the Crawleys in some manner, which was the sole source of her Social Security payments. I have even seen Crawley family reunion pictures where my grandmother is the only Black person in them. My siblings and I all did work for the family as well when we were young.

Thanks to our family's legacy of working for the Crawleys, my grandmother was able to build her modest wooden home first, and later my parents built their USDA-financed house, which was made of blocks.

Before this, Addie Joyce, Fletcher, and the older children had resided in a wooden two-room home with a small kitchen that was situated on a dirt road, also owned by the Crawleys. In fact, it had been one of the Crawley's tenant houses many years before. The primary room in this house had a sofa, chair, table, and Fletcher and Addie Joyce's bed. The kitchen's heat source was an old potbelly stove, and there was an old refrigerator, too. The other room had a bed for the girls and one for the boys. By the time I was three, we were in the newer house, so it was the only childhood home I ever knew.

Although I lived steps from my maternal grandmother for my entire childhood, I had significantly less exposure to my paternal grandparents, seeing my paternal grandmother only every once in a while. The only other memory I have of her is that she was blind in both eyes and wore dark glasses. This would be a genetic condition that would plague me later in my life. I have no memory of my paternal grandfather.

STATE OF ALABAMA, _____ PIKE _____ COUNTY.

KNOW ALL MEN BY THESE PRESENTS:

That W. Douglas Crawley and wife, Wonnie B. Crawley,

for and in consideration of the Sum of One Hundred Dollars and other good and valuable consideration to us in hand paid by Fletcher Robinson, Jr. and Addie P. Robinson

the receipt whereof we do hereby acknowledge, have GRANTED, BARGAINED, AND SOLD, and by these presents do hereby GRANT, BARGAIN, SELL AND CONVEY unto the said

Fletcher Robinson, Jr. and Addie P. Robinson

for and during their joint lives, and upon the death of either of them, then to the survivor of them in fee simple, together with every contingent remainder and right of reversion, the following described Real

Estate, situated in the county of _____ Pike _____ and State of Alabama, to-wit:

Commencing at a point on the East side of Alabama Highway #201 (30 feet from centerline) said point being South 10 deg. 22 min. East 469.2 feet from the intersection of the centerline of said Highway #201 and the centerline of an unpaved county road (This last mentioned point being the Northwest corner of Section 35, Township 10 North, Range 22 East); running thence South 7 deg. 00 min. East 122.0 feet along the East side of Alabama Highway #201; thence North 83 deg. 00 min. East 366.0 feet; thence North 7 deg. 00 min. West 122.0 feet; thence South 83 deg. 00 min. West 366.0 feet to the point of beginning. Said lot lying and being situated in the Northwest quarter of the Northwest quarter of Section 35, Township 10 North, Range 22 East, Pike County, Alabama, and containing 1.02 acres, more or less.

TO HAVE AND TO HOLD, the aforegranted premises to the said Fletcher Robinson, Jr. and Addie P. Robinson for and during their joint lives and upon the death of either of them, then to the survivor of them in fee simple, and to the heirs and assigns of the survivor FOREVER, together with every contingent remainder and right of reversion.

And we do covenant with the said Fletcher Robinson, Jr. and Addie P. Robinson, their assigns, the survivor of them and the heirs and assigns of the survivor, that we are lawfully seized in fee simple of the aforementioned premises; that they are free from all encumbrances; that we have a good right to sell and convey the same to the said Fletcher Robinson, Jr. and Addie P. Robinson their assigns, the survivor of them and the heirs and assigns of the survivor, and that we will WARRANT AND DEFEND THE PREMISES to the said Fletcher Robinson, Jr. and Addie P. Robinson, their assigns, the survivor of them and the heirs and assigns of the survivor forever, against the lawful claims and demands of all persons.

IN WITNESS WHEREOF, we have hereunto set our hands and seals this 3rd day of February, 1969.

SIGNED, SEALED AND DELIVERED IN PRESENCE OF

Robinson's Deed for purchasing land from Douglas and Wonnie Crawley.

The Robinson's Real Estate Mortgage with FHA USDA.

Grandmother, the family matriarch taken during the time she worked inside the Crawley's home.

Thanksgiving 1998 at oldest brother, Jimmy's home.

The Wilson's ranch home purchased after retirement. We were blessed with snow the same year which is unusual for AL.

3

EMMA EXCELS IN SCHOOL

From an early age I enjoyed learning and did well in school. It's important to remember that in this place and time period our schools were desegregated, but that had only happened a few short years earlier, in 1963. I do remember having both African American and white teachers, and in the first grade my best friend was a little white girl.

When I was young, the highest grade you could attend in Banks was ninth grade, at Banks Middle School. From there, the children of families in Banks transitioned to Pike County High School in Brundidge, a considerably larger town with a downtown business district and retail establishments. When the time came, I too transferred to Pike County High School.

In addition to finding a home in the supportive learning environment of school, our faith community was the other one in my life that was pivotal to how my outlook, beliefs, and worldview were formed and developed. We were members of the congregation at Beulah Hill Missionary Baptist Church (BHMBC), which was founded here in Banks in the early 1900s, over a century ago. Multiple generations of my family attended the small church, and it served as the only school for Black people, which is why we are embedded in its history.

I can remember my mother ushering at the ladies' study door. She served as secretary where there are still historical record books with her handwriting. The irony in looking at the financial history of the church is that we had members then tithing 25 cents, and now 3,000 dollars. My mother ensured that my siblings and I were all active there from a young age. We all sang in the choir and participated in all youth activities.

The time right before I was born and when I was a little girl was a volatile period in Alabama's history and the history of America, as African American people rose up to challenge the oppression of Jim Crow. In the early 1960s, the Freedom Rider movement saw integrated groups of Black and white activists ride throughout the state, fighting for equal rights and desegregation. They were terrorized in various ways, from intimidation to targeted violence from the police and angry citizens. The activists' bravery paved the way for progress, but another important thing the Freedom Rides accomplished was to show to the world the racial injustice that was happening in our country.

I'm proud to say that BHMBC also played a role in the

Civil Rights movement. When so many other local churches, including large ones, folded on the request to support the movement, our small church did support it by providing administrative and meeting spaces for activists, as well as a place for them to rest. Church leaders and members were central figures in a concerted effort to register Black voters throughout Pike County in the summer of 1965, in cooperation with clergy and activists from around the country. They tirelessly canvassed countless neighborhoods when it was sweltering, as is typical during the summer in Alabama, and they did it mostly on foot.

The activists were often met with indifference at best, like when they tried to secure a temporary office space in which to do their administrative and organizing work, and blunt, open hostility at worst, as when they endured verbal abuse from the local white power structure. Local citizens who helped them or offered them places to stay were even threatened with losing their jobs once white leaders got wind of what was going on.

Church members consistently dealt with roadblocks when it came to finding places to gather and speak to the many unregistered Black voters in the area, who were still required to take ridiculous literacy and political history tests that white people didn't have to take in order to earn the right to vote. Their system was corrupt beyond belief, and I'm proud that our church took a stand and actively worked for equality for all. Thankfully, the secretary of the group from Robbins, Illinois documented a detailed journal about that summer, so we have a detailed record of what they experienced. Ultimately they were successful in registering many Black voters, but it came at a steep price.

As I entered junior high school, I was a member of the marching band and enrolled in Reserve Officer Training Corp (ROTC). I began playing the flute, which I continued to enjoy throughout high school, and excelled in ROTC. Both activities teach a lot of the same lessons team sports do—foremost discipline, that a group of people, all doing their part, can create something powerful and inspiring. The benefits of these group efforts are not unlike those of a sports team or collaborative professional group. They show us how important keeping our eyes on the collective good can be, as opposed to just concentrating on our own thoughts and actions as individuals.

Excerpt from detailed journal of the Freedom Rider's Movement during the early 1960's.

4

A TROUBLED SOUL

My mother and father didn't have the privilege of receiving much formal education and were working parents at a young age. I'm amazed at what fortitude this required of them, yet they never shirked their family responsibilities. As I mentioned earlier, my mother worked hard to create the best, most loving home she could for us, and we were so lucky to have my grandmother there too, to augment my mother's efforts. We ran back and forth between the two houses and always felt safe, secure, and loved.

My father, Fletcher, had excellent work ethics and toiled every day for us, but sadly he had an alcohol dependency and often what would happen was that he'd work hard all week, only to binge on the weekend and go on a "bender." This addiction caused extreme tension and arguments in our household about finances, arguments, and it impaired the overall health and happiness of our family. The effects of alcoholism were a major source of stress for my mother.

Father's death certificate.

5

TRAGEDY STRIKES

When I was just ten years old and in fifth grade, life as I knew it was completely shattered. My family endured a trauma of such magnitude, it isn't possible to fully recover from it, ever.

As I recall, it was late afternoon or early evening on a Sunday, and my mother and sister were returning home from church. As we heard the car roll in, all of us kids ran out to greet them. It was then that we noticed my father running across the field that abutted the road our house was on. Shock and panic set in at that moment because we realized he was carrying a gun!

My mother had gotten out of the car and was making her way toward my grandmother's house. In the chaos of what erupted, I remember that my middle of three brothers, John, had even grabbed my father's rifle with the intention of protecting my mother from the attack, but it was sadly to no avail. My father threw him to the ground, and this is when all of us children implored Mother to run and try to escape my father, but her response was stunning: "I'm not running anymore."

To our utter horror, Father shot Mother nine times, killing her. She was only 31 years old. To this day, it is of course very difficult to come to terms with these awful memories, and it's quite painful every time I access them. One of the most traumatic lasting memories I have from that day is witnessing my mother fall forward to the ground and noticing the round spots of blood on her back from her many bullet wounds. Being a child and having no understanding of the severity of my mother's injuries whatsoever, I assumed that since the spots were small in diameter, she would probably survive. In reality, the blood pooled below where my mother laid, under her chest and stomach.

The image of the blood spots stayed there for years, long after Mother's body was taken away. In fact, the landmark where she took her last breath is still visible, always a reminder of what had happened that fateful day two decades earlier. It is in the direct path from our family home to my grandmother's house. It's a somber landmark to this day.

After the shooting, my father fled to the woods, but John continued to fight for our mother by throwing a ball at him to try to detain or slow him down in any way he could. The police found my father later that night in the woods and apprehended him, and he asked, "Is my wife OK?" He was convicted and given a lengthy prison sentence—but not as severe as it would have been had he been charged with capital murder.

There was debate in the family when it came to how my father should be charged and what different family members thought his punishment should be: capital murder or life in prison. The debate centered around my grandmother's opinion that capital murder charges usually come with a shorter sentence by death, and my grandmother didn't want my father charged with that because his sentence would be too easy, she thought, not harsh enough. She wanted him to suffer in prison for the remainder of his natural life. My uncle disagreed, on the other hand believing that the problems inherent in our justice system, especially toward Black men, were that drug charges normally carried a longer sentence than murder. Consequently this meant that a capital murder charge did indeed mean that he'd never be freed. Ultimately, my father was released from prison 28 years ago, in 1992, so he served a total of just sixteen years for Mother's murder.

ALABAMA
Center for Health Statistics

STATE OF ALABAMA
CERTIFICATE OF DEATH

29644

STATE FILE NUMBER

TYPE, OR PRINT IN
PERMANENT INK

DECEASED—NAME FIRST: Addie MIDDLE: Joyce LAST: Robinson

DATE OF DEATH (MONTH, DAY, YEAR): November 13, 1977

RACE or COLOR: Black **AGE—LAST BIRTHDAY (YEARS):** 22 **SEX:** F **UNDER 1 YEAR MOS / DAYS:** **UNDER 1 DAY HOURS / MIN.:** **DATE OF BIRTH (MONTH, DAY, YEAR):** 07-17-46 **COUNTY OF DEATH:** Pike

CITY, TOWN, OR LOCATION OF DEATH: Banks-rural 055XX8 **INSIDE CITY LIMITS (SPECIFY YES OR NO):** no **HOSPITAL OR OTHER INSTITUTION—NAME (IF NOT IN EITHER, GIVE STREET AND NUMBER):** Route 1, Banks, Alabama

DECEASED

USUAL RESIDENCE WHERE DECEASED LIVED. IF DEATH OCCURRED IN INSTITUTION, GIVE RESIDENCE BEFORE ADMISSION.

STATE OF BIRTH (IF NOT IN U.S.A., NAME COUNTRY): Alabama **CITIZEN OF WHAT COUNTRY:** U.S.A. **MARRIED, NEVER MARRIED, WIDOWED, DIVORCED (SPECIFY):** Married **SURVIVING SPOUSE (IF WIFE, GIVE MAIDEN NAME):** Fletcher Robinson

SOCIAL SECURITY NUMBER: [redacted] **USUAL OCCUPATION (GIVE KIND OF WORK DONE DURING MOST OF WORKING LIFE, EVEN IF RETIRED):** Machine Operator **KIND OF BUSINESS OR INDUSTRY:** Textile

RESIDENCE—STATE: Alabama 55XX8 **COUNTY:** Pike **CITY, TOWN, or LOCATION:** Banks **INSIDE CITY LIMITS (SPECIFY YES OR NO):** no **STREET AND NUMBER:** Route 1

PARENTS

FATHER—NAME FIRST: John MIDDLE: Pennington LAST: **MOTHER—MAIDEN NAME** FIRST: Addie MIDDLE: Bell LAST: Baskin

PHYSICIAN'S NAME: Alan C. Boothe, Coroner **INFORMANT—NAME:** Charlie Dunn

ADDRESS: Troy, Alabama **ADDRESS:** 101 Arrowhead Drive, Troy, Alabama

CAUSE

MEDICAL CERTIFICATION

IF NO PHYSICIAN WAS IN ATTENDANCE, MEDICAL CERTIFICATION SHOULD BE COMPLETED BY THE LOCAL HEALTH OFFICER, OR CORONER

PART I. DEATH WAS CAUSED BY: (ENTER ONLY ONE CAUSE PER LINE FOR (a), (b), and (c))

IMMEDIATE CAUSE (a): Gunshot wounds to body Cavity (Autopsy performed

DUE TO, OR AS A CONSEQUENCE OF:

CONDITIONS, IF ANY, WHICH GAVE RISE TO IMMEDIATE CAUSE (b): results not available at this time)

DUE TO, OR AS A CONSEQUENCE OF:

STATING THE UNDERLYING CAUSE LAST (c):

965X

APPROXIMATE INTERVAL BETWEEN ONSET AND DEATH: 5-12 Min.

PART II. OTHER SIGNIFICANT CONDITIONS: CONDITIONS CONTRIBUTING TO DEATH BUT NOT RELATED TO CAUSE GIVEN IN PART I (a) **AUTOPSY (YES OR NO):** yes **IF YES, WERE FINDINGS CONSIDERED IN DETERMINING CAUSE OF DEATH:** no 2 **WAS THERE A PREGNANCY IN LAST SIX MONTHS (YES, NO UNKNOWN):** UNK

ACCIDENT, SUICIDE, HOMICIDE, OR UNDETERMINED (SPECIFY): Homicide **DATE OF INJURY (MONTH, DAY, YEAR):** 11—13-77 **HOUR:** Appl:45PM **HOW INJURY OCCURRED (ENTER NATURE OF INJURY IN PART I OR PART II, ITEM 28):** Victim shot several times

INJURY AT WORK (SPECIFY YES OR NO): no **PLACE OF INJURY AT HOME, FARM, STREET, FACTORY, OFFICE BLDG., ETC. (SPECIFY):** home **LOCATION (STREET OR R.F.D. NO., CITY OR TOWN, STATE):** Banks(Rural) Alabama

CERTIFICATION—PHYSICIAN: I ATTENDED THE DECEASED FROM MONTH / DAY / YEAR TO MONTH / DAY / YEAR AND LAST SAW HIM/HER ALIVE ON MONTH / DAY / YEAR **I DID/DID NOT VIEW THE BODY AFTER DEATH:** **DEATH OCCURRED At the place, on the date, and to the best of my knowledge, due to the cause(s) stated**

CERTIFICATION—CORONER OR HEALTH OFFICER: ON THE BASIS OF EXAMINATION OF THE BODY AND/OR ON INVESTIGATION, IN MY OPINION DEATH OCCURRED ON THE DATE AND DUE TO THE CAUSE(S) STATED: **HOUR OF DEATH:** Appx 1:45 PM **THE DECEDENT WAS PRONOUNCED DEAD MONTH:** 11 **DAY:** 13 **YEAR:** 77 **HOUR:** 2:30PM

CERTIFIER

CERTIFIER—PHY, CORONER OR HEALTH OFFICER (TYPE OR PRINT): Alan C. Boothe Coroner 4 **SIGNATURE:** **TITLE:** Coroner **DATE SIGNED (MONTH, DAY, YEAR):** 11-27-77

MAILING ADDRESS—OR STREET OR R.F.D. NO.: 218 Woodland Circle **CITY OR TOWN:** Troy **STATE:** Alabama **ZIP:** 36081

BURIAL

BURIAL, CREMATION, REMOVAL (SPECIFY): Burial **CEMETERY OR CREMATORY—NAME:** Antioch Cemetery **LOCATION:** **CITY OR TOWN:** Troy, Alabama **STATE:**

DATE (MONTH, DAY, YEAR): 11-17-77 **FUNERAL HOME—NAME AND ADDRESS:** Citizen's Chapel, 506 East Academy Street, Troy, Alabama

FUNERAL DIRECTOR'S SIGNATURE: L. M. Grubbs **REGISTRAR'S SIGNATURE:** Etta L. Head **DATE RECEIVED BY LOCAL REGISTRAR:** 11-29-77

Addie Robinson death certificate.

The family Patriarchs and maternal uncles, John T. Pennington and Charlie L Dunn, Sr.

6

THE AFTER EFFECTS OF LOSING ADDIE JOYCE

t's important to remember that on that fateful day when our lives changed forever, my siblings and I really became orphans because we lost both parents—my mother to death, and my father to prison. If it hadn't been for my grandmother, all of us children would have been separated and raised by different relatives or perhaps even placed in foster care.

This is also a time when our school and church communities carried us. I remember the first day I walked back into school after losing my mother, the first thing that happened was that one of my teachers just rushed up to me and enveloped me with her arms. I could feel the empathy and needed it. My siblings and I were all at transitional points in our lives; I was at the cusp of adolescence, and losing our mother, at that moment especially, devastated our worlds.

I also got great support from our school principal, Mr.

John Key, and his wife, a teacher. They were my quiet supporters for years, always willing to bolster me when I very much needed it. In fact, Mr. Key wrote me my very first professional letter of recommendation after I graduated from college.

In some ways, the years after losing my mother were a blur of school, activities, and meeting my future husband, Rodney, but in another way, I realize that I felt my mother's loss acutely with each milestone I reached, from high school graduation to becoming a mother. It's hard not to try to imagine what those years would have been like if we still had my mother's presence and love in our lives.

Trauma is a puzzling thing sometimes. I still remember the chaos of that day, and when I think about and speak of it, chills still run up my back—I really have a visceral reaction. Certain frightening images remain vivid in my mind, and I can access them quickly, but I also have blocked memories out that are too much for me. I have no recollection of my mother's body being covered, the ambulance coming, or where we slept that night—whether it was at our house or our grandmother's house. My oldest sister, Willa, shared with me since writing this book that she initially covered my mother's body not because she thought she had succumbed to her injuries, but she didn't want the dogs to disturb her body in any way. Unfortunately, this highlights the fact that we received no counseling after this trauma, and consequently we never discussed it as a family.

Thankfully, another positive and comforting thing I do remember is a visit from a figure who had been in our community for many years. His name was Willie Mack Kelly. He and his wife were known to be especially spiritual people, and I remember him coming down the road, stopping when he saw the commotion, and immediately taking me in his arms to console me. Moments like these give me comfort, even now.

𝕻ike 𝕮ounty 𝕭oard of 𝕰ducation

Dr. John R. Key
Superintendent of Education

June 6, 1995

Director of Personnel
Duval County Schools
1701 Prudential Drive
Jacksonville, FL 32207-8182

Dear Sir or Madam:

This letter comes as a recommendation for Mrs. Emma Robinson Wilson. I have known Mrs. Wilson for approximately twenty years. In that time I have come to respect both her abilities and her dedication to whatever task is before her. She is quite capable of accomplishing anything she puts her mind to and has shown her commitment to completing what she begins as evidenced by her résumé.

Mrs. Wilson is not afraid of work. She has worked essentially all her life having held a job throughout the time she attended Troy State University while she earned a degree in Mathematics with minors in Computer Science and Business Administration. She also completed a rigorous course for officer training in the United States Army Reserve during the above time period. Mrs. Wilson is currently completing work toward her Masters Degree as well.

Emma's experience on the job as well as her college degrees and background of leadership in the Army Reserve have prepared her very well for a similar leadership position in any area for which she is qualified. Her dedication, perseverance, and willingness to work to accomplish her assigned tasks are qualities which are highly desirable in any applicant for any job and for those being considered as candidates for positions of leadership, the characteristics are virtually indispensable.

It is my pleasure to recommend Mrs. Wilson for any job for which she is qualified. She has certainly proven to me through her actions that she is not only able but also willing to take on any job and achieve the objectives and goals developed by the organization. Should you have any questions regarding this letter, I will be more than glad to answer them.

Sincerely,

John R. Key

John R. Key
Superintendent

JRK:sw

109 East Church Street   Troy, Alabama 36081-2699   Telephone: (334) 566-1850   Fax: (334) 566-2580

Mr. John R. Key wrote Emma's first letter of recommendation.

The Wilson's first family portrait at Murphee Park, Troy, AL. Taken when Rodney was home on leave from Atsugi, Japan.

7

EMMA MEETS HER FUTURE HUSBAND

When I was a young teenager, I noticed a boy, Rodney Wilson, in my history class. One day he sent me a note confessing that he liked me in that special way. It took him a while to win me over, but on the night of my fourteenth birthday we were at a school dance and from that night forward, we considered ourselves a couple. Rodney wasn't a stranger to me, however. He'd been in my orbit for years because one of my mother's best friends lived one house up from his family in Brundidge, a city that's just a short distance from Banks.

My husband has a memory from our earlier childhood that he has shared with me too. It was the Fourth of July, and my family and Annie's family were having fun at Blue Springs State Park. He remembers me being upset and crying when my mother wouldn't allow me to go swimming with the other kids because she feared I'd get hurt. I was the baby and my mother always considered me so. Also, he remembers my mother being so concerned about her baby when I was burnt with coffee that my sister accidentally spilled on my arm. His memory is that she always called me her baby, not my name.

I knew once I had my son that Rodney would be my husband, due to growing up without a father. My goal and priority were for my son to have both his mother and father in his life. I was blessed that Rodney wanted the same things out of life that I wanted. His priority was the same as mine—being a good father to our son, which made it easier to overcome bumps in the road. We were both determined and committed to our son, and he was the focal point that kept us grounded and directed.

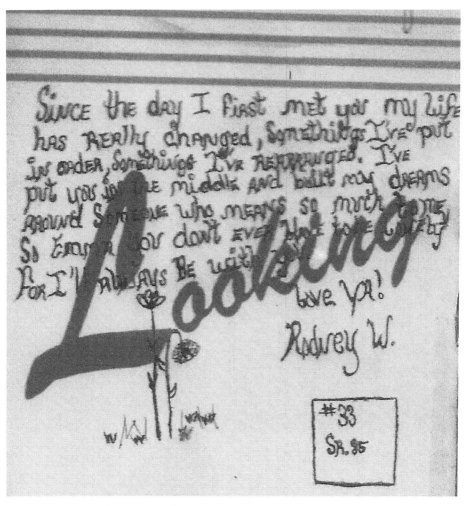

A poem taken from Emma's 1985 Senior Memory Book. This page was reserved for Emma's LIFE PARTNER Rodney Wilson.

Page taken from Emma's 1985 Senior Memory Book. Our commitment as teenagers.

8

A BUMP IN THE ROAD BECOMES A BLESSING

Another event that changed my life forever was becoming pregnant at just fifteen years of age. This isn't what I'd planned, of course, and I was afraid to tell anyone for fear they'd react badly and shame me. I also wondered if Rodney would stand by me through this or abandon me. I just didn't know, so I was worried and afraid.

I finally got up the courage to share the news with my grandmother, and to my surprise and relief, she said she already knew and could just tell what was going on with me. She had lots of life experience and wisdom, which older Black people call "mother wit," so perhaps I shouldn't have been shocked that she knew. She supported me, just like she always did, but I'd find out what that really meant after I had the baby.

My oldest brother Jimmy, expressed his deep disappointment, and so did one of my uncles, but ultimately my family and brothers and sisters were there for me throughout my pregnancy and after the birth of our son. I also know that some of the older members in our church talked in a judgmental way about my situation, but I knew that my top priority needed to be focusing on creating a positive future for my baby, which is exactly what I did.

I was lucky that I felt very well throughout my pregnancy, and it went smoothly with no complications or problems. Once it came time to have the baby, I received a spinal tap to ease my labor pains. Fortunately, I had my son when we were out of school during Christmas break, which prevented me from having to miss school. Other than that, I have few memories of the birth.

Rodney's and my beautiful son, Douglas Norris Wilson, was born on December 22, 1983 at a healthy nine pounds, eleven ounces. The challenge at this time was that Rodney was living with his mother in Pittsburgh, Pennsylvania. I not only had to inform him about the pregnancy over the telephone, but he wasn't there with me when Douglas was born. I definitely felt fortunate to have my family surrounding me and supporting me through my pregnancy and birth, though. Fortunately, Rodney returned to Brundidge the summer after Douglas was born with the determination to be present instead of absent, to be a role model, and to model a good father instead of just speaking of what a good father should do. He returned home and did just that.

Rodney and Emma Pike 2018 NAACP Black Tie Banquet.

Douglas "Norris" Wilson and his father at the 2003 graduation from Samuel W. Wolfson High School.

4th of July celebration at the ranch.

Farm life on the ranch.

9

A LIFE CHANGE AND
A LIFE PARTNER

I will say with utmost certainty that having Douglas was the thing that turned my young life around and caused me—nearly immediately and irrevocably—to grow up and intentionally decide to be as strong a role model to him as I could. In other words, what some may have considered an unwelcome surprise, I chose to embrace and set out to let motherhood be a guiding light in my life. He was my azimuth that always directed my path. I wanted to work hard to give Douglas a good life and to give him things I never had, from financial resources to a certain stability that, once my mother was taken away and my father imprisoned, was hard for me to feel, even though my grandmother took wonderful care of us.

I also wondered whether Rodney would stand by me. Well, he did, and we really grew up together. We married and Rodney transformed into the man Douglas and I needed him to be. Throughout our life, which has seen us live in many different places, both in the United States and internationally, Rodney took care of us. He has been my rock and the cornerstone of our family, unquestionably.

From the time Douglas was born, I took my role as his caregiver seriously. I treasured the duties of preparing his bottles, comforting him when he was upset, and doting on him in general. I felt flattered when my grandmother complimented me about how I cared for him. We were so connected that when I tried to place Douglas in daycare he was inconsolable every time I dropped him off, even though my older sister Willa worked there. After that, my grandmother came through in a big way and cared for him while I went back to school.

Another realization I came to after Douglas' birth was an even steelier determination to complete my higher education, whatever it took. Even then, I knew education was the ticket to better, higher paying work and to attaining our version of the American Dream.

My sister Dianna influenced my decisions when it came to pursuing my higher education and opting for a military career. I watched her attend college by working at McDonald's full time, earning student loans and grants, and then joining the military, so those were big drivers for me. I decided I wanted to follow those paths too, though I knew it wasn't going to be easy doing those things with a baby.

I received grants and secured loans to attend college, as well, and finally finished paying them off after nineteen long years, in 2009. This is an issue I speak about later in the book, the crushing debt students take on now in order to get higher education degrees. It was doable for someone my age, though it still took a long time to pay the loans back, but each year it becomes less and less feasible for young people. This is a shame, because I consider education to be the great equalizer. Advanced training prepares young people for better-paying jobs, but it's becoming harder and harder to get with each passing year.

I set some aggressive goals for myself once I graduated from high school. First, I joined the army reserves and went through eight weeks of basic training in Fort Jackson, South Carolina. The following year I did Subsistence Food Supply Advanced Instruction Training (AIT) in Fort Lee, Virginia. That was a thirteen-week stint. My grandmother cared for Douglas throughout both of those periods.

I then registered at Troy State University (TSU), now known as Troy University (TU), and in the meantime I had also decided that I wanted to become an army officer, which would require special army reserve officer training (ROTC). Unfortunately, TSU didn't offer ROTC training, so in order to get around that I registered as a dual enrollment at Auburn University's Montgomery (AUM) campus and TSU.

I took two afternoon classes typically at TSU and then attended morning classes two days a week at Auburn, which was about an hour-and-a-half commute each way from Banks. My life was a bit of a blur at this point, I was so busy and going in so many directions at this point! It was a demanding time, but I kept my eye on the prize: creating the best life possible for my family.

After completing my ROTC training, I emerged as a second lieutenant and was commissioned as a reserve quartermaster officer rather than going on active duty. At this time, Rodney was involved in serving our country as well. He had joined the National Guard and trained in Fort Knox, Kentucky. Being that the National Guard wasn't providing the future Rodney had planned for us, he decided to join the navy. Rodney and I agreed that since he was on active duty, my being in the reserve would enable me to care for Douglas.

In college, my concentrations were in the areas of public administration and computer science, and I later earned my BS in mathematics with a double minor in business administration and computer science. I wanted to study practical subjects and gain skills that would be transferable to many potential professional positions, as well as make me a competitive candidate in the job market.

I have always been a big goal setter, but I don't allow myself to become overwhelmed. I methodically reached my goals by breaking them down into smaller pieces. Then they aren't so daunting.

Troy University Graduation 1991.

Meet the Wilson family: Rodney, Douglas, Emma, Kamiyah, Pasha and Sevyn (not pictured) Wilson.

10

MILITARY SERVICE MEANS
A NOMADIC LIFE

Rodney's active duty status meant that we usually weren't in one place for too long. Sometimes he went to an assignment unaccompanied, and other times Douglas and I accompanied him. Each arrangement offered unique challenges. When Rodney went by himself to serve, the long separations were hard on our family. When he'd come home on leave, I could feel things getting tense as he prepared to return to his post.

Seeing him leave was quite difficult for both Douglas and me, and it was also hard not to have Rodney there consistently with us during those times in terms of raising Douglas. Rodney had to miss certain milestone moments, and that was hard. For example, he was in Japan for two years, from 1992 to 1994. That's a significant amount of time to miss together as a family.

Like many military families, we became experts at moving because of so many relocations. I learned how to plan, pack, and execute a move with military precision—pardon the pun! It's interesting though, because you also learn what things make a new locale feel like home fairly quickly. I am supremely organized, even to the point of being "a lot OCD," and it may sound like that's something I would have picked up being in the military, but I actually come by it naturally. My father was very precise and organized, and I definitely get it from him, and a couple of my siblings have these traits as well.

Emma's ROTC Military Ball at Auburn University, Montgomery, AL.

(Top Left: Emma, Rodney's mother, Margaret, Douglas & Rodney) Riding horses and camels at the Pyramids of Giza, Cairo Egypt.

11

AN EXPANSIVE CAREER MARKED BY ACHIEVEMENT

I n 1995 we moved to Jacksonville, Florida, where Rodney worked on two naval bases and became a commissioned officer, which required that he go for a training stint in Rhode Island. He was also stationed during this period at Parris Island Marine Corps Recruit Depot in South Carolina.

Meanwhile, I worked for seven years teaching mathematics at Samuel W. Wolfson High School. My average class size numbered anywhere between 32 and 40 students, and I would say that during this period is when I made the realization that I had identified what I really loved to do. I found teaching to be incredibly rewarding and fulfilling in multiple ways—I received great satisfaction from enabling students to make a discovery that excited them, or arrive at that "aha" moment of understanding. I developed wonderful relationships with my students, as evidenced by their high level of achievement in the standardized math tests.

I am proud to say that their scores consistently impressed me—a whopping 80 percent of my students scored at or above grade level. I believe the reason for this had to do with the fact that, aside from my classroom teaching, I made myself available to my students at other times, offered after and before school tutoring, and tried to do all I could to accommodate their varied learning styles.

Looking back on this experience, I'd say that teaching was the work I most loved, but it was also the hardest work I ever did by far. Still, the rewards were worth it and outweighed the challenges considerably. Between administrative constraints, the complex family issues that my students contended with, and the challenges posed by trying to teach many students whose needs were all different, teaching presented me with real dilemmas, but at the end of the day I knew I was giving my students all that I had to offer and preparing them well for their futures in whatever line of work or higher learning they chose.

I also learned while teaching that I had a knack for effective classroom management. Students entered my classroom with all kinds of problems, from learning and behavioral disabilities to a host of other different challenges to include poverty, but I dealt with each and every one of them as an individual and addressed their unique needs. This didn't mean I compromised when it came to what I demanded of them, however. I had high expectations, and for the most part they tried to live up to them.

I found that I had a particular talent for effective classroom management, which means keeping the classroom under good control and students learning, despite behavioral challenges, administrative demands, and other distractions. I ended up excelling in this area—and enjoying it so much—that I mentored peer teachers on the topic, and that was quite fulfilling.

In 2003, we got an opportunity that was life-changing in many ways. Rodney was assigned to work in Cairo, Egypt, and since Douglas was out of the house and attending the Air Force Academy in Colorado at that point, we decided that there was no reason I shouldn't accompany him there. This ended up being a rich learning experience, a cultural adventure, and an amazing professional opportunity for me, all rolled into one.

While in Egypt, I worked as the housing manager for the United States embassy, supervising the 246-unit housing pool that consisted of 149 short-term leases, one long-term lease, fifteen government-owned villas, plus four government-owned apartment complexes with 77 residential units. The job entailed vast responsibility, which included acquiring and assigning housing for incoming Department of State personnel. I was the primary liaison between the American embassy, Egyptian landlords, Egyptian municipalities, supply and property management, facilities, the regional security office, and the post-occupational safety and health office. Additionally, I was responsible for the complete move-in process (cleanliness of residential units, and they had to be properly furnished and equipped with all appliances and accessories) and managed all aspects of leasing (negotiation of new and renewal leases, termination of any problematic leases), preparation and submission of waivers, troubleshooting of problems and complaints from tenants and landlords, and coordinated approval on oversized or overpriced units from the Department of State, Washington, DC. I also took on the revision of a lengthy and highly detailed military housing handbook. I worked to place a record number of families in needed housing very rapidly and efficiently. It was a logistics-heavy position, and I enjoyed keeping all the moving parts of such an expansive effort going at the right speeds. This valuable experience prepared me for the work I do now with the company my husband and I own, Rapid Acquisitions Management Solutions, or RAMS.

Living in Egypt was a rich cultural experience too. Rodney and I had a lovely place in which to live, household help, and we became adept at communicating with food vendors and learning how to cook typical Egyptian meals that were quite different from what we were used to in the United States.

As is typical when you're in the military, you don't remain anywhere for too long usually, so the following year in 2004 we returned home and settled in Maryland, living at times in Bethesda and Rockville. Rodney's next set of orders saw him serve overseas in Iraq for a year. During that time, I moved to an apartment that was close to the Pentagon where I enjoyed my next professional opportunity as a senior operations analyst for Quantum Research International. At that point, I was mobilized into active duty to support Operation Iraqi Freedom (OIF) and Operation Enduring Freedom (OEF), which was a military response to 2001's September 11 attacks.

My next position was working as a transportation liaison officer at the Pentagon's Army Logistics Operation Center, where I was responsible for tracking all personnel and equipment intra- and inter-transportation movements for OIF/OEF.

I then served as a logistic automation systems expert. Primarily responsible for retrieving and analyzing data using the army's suite of automated readiness tools (Joint Operations Programming and Execution System, Single Mobility System, Army Readiness Management System, Property Book Unit Supply Enhanced, Army Flow Model, Logistics Integrated Warehouse, United States Army Force Management Agency, Mobiliction Deployment Integrated System, Force Requirements Enhanced Database, FEDLOG, Electronic Joint Manpower and Personnel System, Master Personnel System, Worldwide Individual Augmentee System, Army Training Requirements and Resource System, and Department of the Army Mobilization System). Following this, I was the chief operations planner in the

Office of the Deputy Chief of Staff at the United States Army Headquarters in Washington, DC. I worked on infrastructure risk management projects and was involved with creating an influenza management plan and other logistical project plans. I felt fortunate to be able to collaborate closely with the Director of Logistics and Operations. I gained valuable professional experience in each of the successive positions in my military career. Each prepared me for my next set of duties.

From 2009 to 2010, I was a human resources manager at MacDill Air Force Base in Tampa, Florida. While there, I coordinated with Theater Joint Task Force commanders to ensure trained and ready personnel were top priority. We worked to enhance our training procedures and projects having to do with workplace safety and compliance, monitored army-wide tasking of Theater Army Individual Augmentation requirements, and provided monthly projections of personnel files, developed and coordinated policies governing Individual Mobilization Augmentee and fiscal responsibility, developed a vision which aligned performance expectations with organizational goals, and ensured equal opportunity principles were adhered to throughout the organization and in compliance with applicable laws.

After Rodney's retirement in 2009 and our return to Alabama, I was employed as a contractor with Sigmatech in 2011 as a United States Army operations planner for the

Security Assistance Command in Huntsville. I planned and facilitated various studies and projects. I updated staff on vital issues and performed key operations and logistics work.

The skills I gained from my military career were so varied, and as I mentioned before, they all built upon each other and helped me as I reentered the civilian work world. Joining the military allowed me to experience life in many different places, which taught me so much, too. In retrospect, those years flew by, and in some ways, it felt like before Rodney and I knew it, we were back home in Alabama, ready to start a new chapter.

Auburn University Montgomery, first year cadet.

Jacksonville, FL 2003 Samuel W Wolfson High School Graduation. Emma's last year teaching before moving to Cairo, Egypt.

12

RETIRING FROM THE MILITARY AND VENTURING INTO REAL ESTATE INVESTING

Our time in Cairo changed us in many ways, and an important one was that this period allowed Rodney and I to revisit a goal that we had talked about decades before as a young couple. We had long dreamed of investing in real estate, but started to consider it more seriously while we lived in Egypt. My work had given us an up-close look at the ins and outs of property management through working as a housing manager with the City of Troy Housing Authority and the Cairo, Egypt embassy. At this point, we started to redefine our life's work upon returning to Alabama so that it focused on giving back to our community somehow. We wanted the period following the completion of our military careers to be about helping people and allowing them the opportunity to have something that everyone deserves from the get-go, but doesn't always get: an affordable, decent home where they can raise their children.

Rodney set a goal for us of earning 10,000 dollars per month from real estate investments as soon as possible after retiring from the military. Not ones to shy away from challenges, we dove in. Part of the reason we decided real estate would be the best bet for us was that we felt it was a safer investment than other more volatile options like the stock market. We also kept returning to the idea that we wanted to go back to the community we were raised in and give back by investing in it. There was definitely a need for affordable, quality housing in Pike County, and we wanted to fill that need.

I strongly believe that every child deserves to grow up in a clean, safe, and pleasant environment, because if you don't get a start like that in life, you don't even know it's possible to aspire to it. For example, when we considered what kinds of properties to invest in, we prioritized buying single detached homes with yards, so there would always be a place for the children to play. We also concentrated on purchasing solid, site-built homes rather than fabricated homes, because these homes depreciate in value as time goes on, while single-family detached structures appreciate.

We were especially concerned with giving our future tenants' children the opportunity to have a safe place to play outside. In housing projects, children are often kept inside because the communal areas are unsafe due to criminal activity. I had a unique understanding of this need because years ago, through my work with the Public Housing Authority, I saw the realities of what challenges residents were up against first-hand. In addition to younger families with children, Rodney and I also wanted to offer affordable housing solutions to others in need, such as handicapped individuals, older community members, and veterans.

After we came to these decisions, we set out to look for our first investment property to buy. We found two "fixer uppers" in Brundidge and then we took the plunge. Initially we spent 32,000 dollars and invested about the same amount of money to renovate them. We were fortunate to know the local contractors who we hired to perform the renovations and believed we could trust them. It was also gratifying to provide work and invest in our home community in that way too.

Rodney and I were quite strategic and risk-averse in our approach to real estate investing. We settled on the decision that we would never carry more than one outstanding mortgage in addition to that of our own home, so we would never feel overextended financially or put ourselves at risk for becoming potential victims of a sudden economic downturn. We also wanted to live in a way where things weren't so tight that we didn't have discretionary money for activities and travel, and to assist family members financially if they experienced some type of crisis or emergency. As we have seen over the last year of 2020, one's economic reality can turn on a dime if there is sudden mass unemployment, layoffs, and other unstable factors that overtake the economy.

Over a period of years, we gradually accrued more properties, so that we now have a seventeen-property real estate portfolio, and this doesn't include our own wonderful home in Goshen, Alabama that we bought after retiring from the military, when we were just in our early 40s. Rodney retired in 2009, and I followed him into retirement four years later, in 2013.

We are incredibly grateful to have found our dream retirement home, which consists of a beautiful ranch home, guest house, warehouse storage building, and a barn, in addition to fields to raise our horses and cows. We knew for sure that we would have horses and cows, because Rodney has a lifelong love of riding. We also raise cows that we sell periodically for meat. Similar to our real estate goals, having a home base like the one we have is something Rodney and I talked about and envisioned since we were teens.

Rapid Acquisition Management Solutions serve as outreach to the community.

Rapid Acquisition Management Solutions advertisement ad for 2019.

Horses on the ranch (Diamond, Samear, Major and Blaze). Blaze was born on the ranch.

Welcomed a new Calf to the ranch.

God blessed us with our dream home that we spoke of as teenagers.

13

EMMA AND RODNEY'S POST-RETIREMENT DREAM: GIVE BACK TO THEIR COMMUNITY

As Rodney and I tried to imagine our life after retiring from the military, we always returned to the fact that it was a big priority for both of us to return to Alabama, where we grew up, and throw our energies into doing work that could really change the lives of the folks in our own community. We developed the idea to start our company, Rapid Acquisitions Management Solutions, LLC, or RAMS, and founded it in 2010.

I serve as the chief executive officer of RAMS, and our uncompromising professional standards include complete responsiveness to our clients and their goals, the ability to adapt to their changing needs, and a relentless pursuit of efficiency and excellence. I am proud that RAMS is a woman, minority, service connected veteran-owned small business. As such, we strive to do the best for our clients and actively support local small business initiatives.

At its inception, RAMS' mission was expansive and included providing a wide range of services for both the federal government and commercial sectors, like public relations services, staffing solutions, health information management, logistics assistance, strategic planning, and educational support services. Rodney and I wanted to use the experiences we gained throughout our lengthy military careers and build on all that with RAMS, as well as siphon all the energy from our new initiative right back into our beloved community. Another interest of ours was to offer educational services to local students. We had significant backgrounds working in all of these realms and more, so we pictured RAMS being a "one-stop shop" in a sense, for clients in need of all of these types of services.

RAMS is housed in a roomy brick office building very near to downtown Troy that houses our administrative offices, meeting spaces that we offer to local organizations, and an area for tutoring services that we offer students. We are blessed to have this building for many reasons.

This is a good time to state a philosophy that I have found to be true. Though I might have an idea of how things are going to be in terms of what my goals are or plans that Rodney and I have formulated, I firmly believe that God's plan is the master plan, and that despite what we may have in mind for how things are supposed to evolve, He puts exactly the right people, circumstances, and opportunities in front of us just when we need them—even if we don't realize at the time that they are the best things for us.

The way RAMS grew and developed is a perfect example of this. It has turned out that the bulk of what we provide to the community are educational offerings for children and adults in our community, and we serve as a place of connection for many local organizations, as they use our spaces for meetings. Our property management arm is still going strong, and we continue to provide high-quality housing for people in need, but we also offer financial management workshops and educate first-time home buyers. We help to ensure that the many steps they go through to buy a house go smoothly, from getting knowledge about their credit rating and securing pre-approval for a mortgage, to understanding what home ownership entails, like maintaining your property and being engaged in your community.

A RAMS initiative that is very near and dear to my heart is the two-week summer math lab that we offer to students at no charge. We teach lower-level math and pre-algebra to participants, and this not only strengthens their skills, it prevents the learning backslide that we know happens for kids in the summer when they're not in a learning environment consistently. We also offer math tutoring for local students throughout the academic year.

In addition to leading RAMS, I'm deeply committed to civic involvement and being an active member of my long-time spiritual home, the BHMBC in Banks. In addition to being my home church, it played a great part in my mother's life. She got much fulfillment from being part of the congregation when she was alive. Despite living in so many places over many years that were far from Banks, I never gave up my membership in the congregation and always tithed to them. Since BHMBC is historic, Rodney and I also supported a project to preserve the integrity of the structure.

We were happy to commit ourselves to the renovation of the church, which ultimately was a 350,000 dollar project. Rodney served as the project manager for the complex project, and I served as the financial accounting officer. We were fortunate to be able to offer space in our RAMS office building to our church so they could hold services and church meetings there for the twelve-month period when the remodeling project was going on.

It was a fulfilling process to watch the church's sanctuary, kitchen, and group spaces transform. We held a rededication ceremony and celebration in 2019 upon the project's completion, and it was a joyous experience. I feel that we were able to honor the many who came before us at the church. They worked hard to establish it, and the church has always been a beacon for its congregation and community, also serving as a school for local children in its early years.

Emma with sister Dianna at Pike NAACP 2018 Black Tie Banquet.

Commitment: When your belief is strong and your purpose just, when no obstacle can stand in your way.

Destiny: The choices you make in life ultimately determine your destiny.

Beulah Hill Missionary Baptist Church before and after exterior renovations.

14

TAKING ADVERSITY AND
TURNING IT INSIDE OUT

I have realized that I feel called to share my story because, while my life has been punctuated by formidable challenges, it is how I responded to those tests that has made all the difference. Failing at some point in your life is inevitable, but how you respond is more important, and not giving up. When you lose your dear mother to homicide at your father's hands, or have an unplanned pregnancy as a teenager as I did, one option is to allow those events to define you in a negative way. You may consciously, or even subconsciously, decide that setting goals to achieve and enjoy a stable, joyful, and prosperous future life is simply an impossible dream. You think, if this happened to me, how can I imagine anything good for my future, and believe in my heart that I truly deserve it?

I want people to take from my story that no matter what challenges you are given, you can overcome them—even be strengthened by them—and go on to lead a productive, happy, and very full life. You can seek new experiences and actively expand your world because, yes, we all deserve it. Obstacles should not turn into excuses for failing to advance in life, and I believe I am living proof of that. Growing up economically disadvantaged as a child, losing my mother, and being a teen mother very well could have broken me and caused me to stagnate, but I didn't allow it.

It's important to think of what it means to powerfully and successfully rise to challenges, and all that it requires: determination, clarity, and steering clear of victim mentality. I set my sights on a future that was unlimited, painted my own portrait of the American dream, and made it a reality.

There is no quick or easy trick to transforming your life. If fate has thrown some unfortunate arrows at you, or you've made some choices you now wish you hadn't, this doesn't mean that you can't imagine and strive for a better life. Something I didn't expect was to be dealing with eye and sight problems because of a hereditary cornea problem. I've now had three corneal transplants and throughout my recoveries from those, and dealing with impaired eyesight, I have needed to adapt and remain positive. You have to take a long-haul, one-day-at-a-time approach, and all the smaller goals you set eventually become sizable ones. The old cliché "Rome wasn't built overnight and brick by brick" applies.

What I've learned over my lifetime regarding setbacks and obstacles has made me passionate about helping others, especially at-risk children. It is often difficult for them to picture a semblance of a positive future for themselves if they've never known anything but poverty, a chaotic family life, and failing in school. It's hard to have hope when these harsh realities and circumstances have surrounded you your entire life. How can they even construct dreams for the future and picture feeling happy and secure about their place in the world when they've wanted for the basics, like a comfortable, safe home environment and a family support structure that is unshakeable. What I hope for the children who are being raised in the homes Rodney and I own is that they can allow themselves the luxury of dreaming.

That said, I don't subscribe to a 100 percent "pull yourself up by the bootstraps" mentality, either. We can't look away or ignore the certain realities, like systemic racism, which is sadly alive and well in our schools, workplaces, and our American justice system. As a teacher and now a tutor through my RAMS work, I see the effects of our deeply flawed systems on the kids of color who we work with.

Take early childhood education, for instance. This is something I'm quite concerned about because I believe—and studies back this belief—that it's critical for children ages two to four years of age to be in some sort of structured preschool learning environment out of the home. Aside from preparing them for kindergarten, they need that social head start of being able to be away from home for a certain number of hours per day and interaction with their peers. It's during those years that they learn how to line up, sit still in the classroom, and get their rudiments of learning down: learning their alphabet, numbers, colors, and other foundational things that prepare them to enter school on a level playing field with other children.

As a teacher, I witnessed with my own eyes the serious problems that early inequities sow. If a child starts having reading problems early, for example, by the time they're in third grade they then won't be able to properly understand even the instructions on a math test, so this one deficit causes untold damage to their education and limits them in so many ways. We know, for example, that poverty and missing out on getting a good educational start has been linked to everything from poorer health in adulthood and lower earning potential to a higher likelihood of dropping out of high school or being incarcerated.

When children don't get that leg up that preschool provides, they start out behind their peers and fall further and further behind as their educations progress, and they never do catch up. It is sad to say but sometimes they are doomed from the start. I know this from experience too, because my father could not read or write. Perhaps this is part of why I feel so passionate about making sure that young, disadvantaged children are fully prepared to excel in school.

As I mentioned before, our justice system also perpetuates racial inequalities. Warehousing is really the only way to describe the mass incarceration of Black men in America.

They consistently get harsher sentences for less serious crimes, like possession of marijuana.

My family knows first-hand about how broken the justice system is as well, because my father served less time for murder than my brother did for a drug charge. My brother was sentenced to 70 years in prison for drug charges, but ended up serving eleven years and being on probation for nineteen, whereas my father served just sixteen years in prison for ending my mother's life and was eligible for parole repeatedly prior to sixteen years but denied due to some family opposition.

The fact that having an arrest record blackballs you and so permanently mars your future is very unjust, I believe. A prime example of this is that if you commit a felony and even finish serving your sentence, you will be branded and judged forever, have lifelong difficulties getting a job, and be barred from voting. I consider this widespread jailing of Black men to be a modern day form of slavery. Again, educational opportunity is key in helping us avoid the "prison pipeline" for our youth.

Tragedy, mistakes and hardship will come, what's important is what you do next...

Rodney and I celebrating New Years Eve, Downtown Montgomery.

15

SYSTEMIC RACISM'S EFFECT ON MY LIFE

As a Black woman in my 50s, I have my own stories about how systemic racism has impacted me, my husband, and our son. As a young woman, one of the early jobs I applied to after graduating from college was the assistant executive director position with the Troy Housing Authority. The executive director interviewed me, we had a great conversation, and she seemed impressed with me. I was well qualified and connected to the community. Ultimately, I was not selected for the position because the previous executive director—my interviewer's predecessor— knew someone else who was being interviewed for the job and nepotism prevailed.

Despite the fact that the other candidate had significantly less experience than me, he was hired. Fortunately, the executive director was disturbed about the injustices of the selection and did something about it. She went ahead and decided to create a completely new position at the Housing

Authority and offered it to me, with a salary that was considerably more than I was earning at my current position with the County Extension Service. These types of painful, eye-opening experiences happen all the time, and they are discouraging, though I never wavered in my determination to keep trying for advancement in my career.

The same thing happened decades later upon returning to Alabama from active duty and retiring from the military. This time I applied for the executive director position at the same Housing Authority. Obviously, being a seasoned professional, my education, knowledge, and experience over the course of my career, along with obtaining my housing manager certificate from the same agency, should have put me in the place of being offered this position, or at least ranking as a top candidate. The credential was even one of the educational requirements for the job. However, again someone with considerably less experience and qualifications was selected for the job.

We also conveyed to our son, Douglas, about the importance of higher education and encouraged him to pursue it. He earned a bachelor's degree from Florida State University and a master's degree from TU. We believed that these educational accomplishments would put him ahead and give him a competitive edge when he was out in the job market looking for work. However, he has seen that, despite having these degrees, he still receives a lower salary than his white counterparts who don't have degrees.

This lived injustice has made him say that he wishes he would have gone to trade school instead of college because of the large debt he took on in order to get his education. He is also considering encouraging his own children to pursue a trade route other than college or graduate school, not only because of the level of debt they would incur—and who knows how high tuition will be then—but he feels that he hasn't received great measurable benefits from his higher education. It's a slap in the face really, and even though it took me years to pay back my college student loans, the amount of debt is so much higher today for students, it's impeding them from being able to do things like buy a house or start a family.

Thinking of these societal problems brings me to the topic of just raising a Black son in this country and the dilemma it presents to parents. Like all Black parents, we had to counsel Douglas on how to behave when he was out in public in order to stay safe. Rodney did a wonderful job teaching our son how to conduct himself in the world as a Black man. This came down to how he looked and what energy he put forth in the world, especially what he should do and say in case he was stopped by the police for any reason. When Douglas was a teen and young man, I remember feeling overwhelming worry and praying a lot whenever he would leave the house. This worry wasn't only for Douglas; I worried about Rodney just as much because as a Black man you are guilty because you are

Black. A simple unwarranted or warranted police stop for a headlight can escalate to someone dying.

It's hard to accurately describe the weight of this stress on generations and generations of Black families, and the fact that we are still living this reality in 2021 is the best evidence that not just awareness but action is needed to successfully begin dismantling these systems and practices.

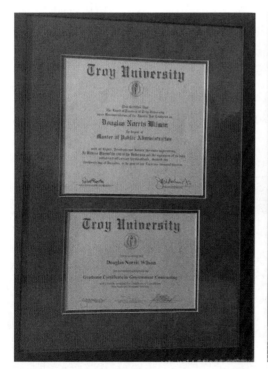

Douglas states, he hasn't received great measurable benefits from his higher education because, despite having these degrees, he still receives a lower salary than his white counterparts who don't have degrees.

16

HEALTHCARE INEQUITIES AND ITS IMPACT ON OUR COMMUNITIES

I think many people are frustrated by the state of healthcare in our country, but people of color suffer the most from the effects of being underinsured and uninsured, and are even less likely to get pain relief when hospitalized. Black women are two to three times more likely than white women to die due to pregnancy-related causes[1], a fact which is as astounding as it is shameful, and our community experiences serious chronic conditions like diabetes and stroke at astronomical rates. COVID-19 has only exacerbated these realities, and it has opened a Pandora's box that is filled with all the ugly flaws in our health system, economic inequality, and structures that hurt people of color. This extends to the fact that the majority of our country's essential workers are also people

---

1   https://www.necn.com/news/local/black-women-are-2-to-3-times-more-likely-to-die-from-pregnancy-related-causes-heres-why/2404214/

of color, and we experience much higher rates of serious COVID-19 illness, hospitalization, and death as compared to the white population.[2] Why?

Essential workers perform such important tasks that allow our society to keep running, like working in grocery stores, post offices, schools, and restaurants, yet they are also the most economically affected by the pandemic. These are the individuals who don't have the option to work remotely, who don't have the option to social distance at home, who cannot stay home because they don't have leave to cover their pay, and who don't feel comfortable going to the doctor even if they feel sick for fear of losing their jobs. These workers, who are most at risk of being exposed to the virus, have long deserved higher pay for the work they do, in my opinion, but the need is even more urgent now as we grapple with the devastating effects of COVID-19 in our families and communities.

We want to develop some services at RAMS in the future for families who are struggling as they deal with pandemic-related disparities. Low-income families often have spotty Wi-Fi or none at all; this directly and negatively impacts their children's learning, since virtual learning and online classes are the norm now for the foreseeable future.

We're also learning that if a household doesn't have a laptop or reliable device that a child can use, they can't participate fully in learning, and if their parents haven't

---

2   https://www.epi.org/publication/black-workers-covid/

acquired the computer skills necessary to help them solve technological issues that typically occur during the average school day, that can derail a child's learning as well. These issues have definitely added a new level of stress to the lives of the families we work with.

We hope to offer one-on-one remote support for students doing school remotely and for those who might not even have a parent at home during the school day since they must work. The pandemic exposed a whole new set of inequalities for these families, and I feel as if they are forgotten. Our plan is for RAMS to be able to step in and help in this area somehow as well.

Sometimes it seems that people want to look away from these issues, but we can't afford to anymore. I believe we must tackle them head on and commit ourselves to doing everything we can as citizens to equalize opportunity for all children, which means being engaged with our communities, helping our neighbors, and voting.

17

WE ALL PLAY AN IMPORTANT PART IN HOLDING EACH OTHER UP

I have always tried to live my life grounded in faith and hope, and understood early on that God's plan always contains things that surprise us. I enjoy counseling and motivating young people on how they can set big goals and achieve them if they believe they can. I have tried to do this type of work ever since I taught in Florida and now at RAMS. I have done motivational speaking for teen mothers, and I share how my early pregnancy became a motivator in my life to better myself, rather than a disadvantage. Indeed, it became my most powerful motivator. With young people that I can share words with, I tell my own story to them and the odds I was up against as a young person, but they can see that I'm living proof that I overcame them, and so can they. I stress to them my belief that there are very few mistakes that you cannot recover from.

Memories of my mother still fuel my drive, even all these years later. Although the grief never disappears from a trauma such as this, I feel that I channeled it in healthy ways that have served me well. I was shaped by the love of my mother, and that lives on today and helped me to prioritize Douglas always and give him the life that I couldn't have— that is certainly a blessing and brings me joy.

My personal trauma also made me face how I would deal with my anger toward my father and handle my relationship with him. My father applied for parole many times over the years he spent in prison for the murder of my mother and was repeatedly rejected, but was released after sixteen years because he developed congestive heart failure.

He returned to Pike County, and I had to prepare myself emotionally for the fact that I would likely be running into him on a regular basis. I could have chosen bitterness, but I opted to make peace with what his release meant for all of us children. I ultimately helped him find a place to live because I was working for the Housing Authority. He lived there for many years until his death in 2013.

I could have chosen to embrace bitterness for him during the remainder of his life, but I also had to examine my values as a Christian and act accordingly. I have found that this approach helped with my own closure that I sought around the death of my mother.

I will never tire of thinking about how we can all work toward the ideal that I hold dear: our world must be one that invests in all of its children equally, no matter where they come from or their zip code, because they are all so deserving of the same chance to access life's opportunities. Family, friends, neighbors, teachers, clergy, and all types of mentors are vitally important in shaping every life, including mine.

Even though I cite my personal determination in meeting my goals, I am very aware of who the angels have been in my life that were there at pivotal moments to cheer me on: my mother, my siblings, especially Dianna, my grandmother, my mother's brothers, Uncle John Pennington, who was a father figure for me and Charlie L. Dunn, Rodney, who has maintained unshakeable strength in his commitment to our family, Douglas, my BHMBC family, my teachers, many professional mentors, and more. We all need people in our lives who will share and support us in our disappointments as well as our successes, because life is full of both.

There's nothing more accurate than that oft-said truism, "It takes a village to raise a child." I saw this in action during my youth, despite the tragedy that disrupted it, and I have continued to see it throughout my life, no matter where I've lived or what I was doing. We need that village to surround us throughout our entire lives, and we must always be part of that village for others.

Robinson siblings family portrait Fourth of July 2010.

CLOSING THOUGHTS

The more life experiences I have, the stronger my belief becomes that our challenges can propel us rather than hold us back. Mine certainly contributed to what some would say was a "sky's the limit" attitude. Education and joining the military allowed me to expand my world, identify opportunities, and go to places—literally and figuratively—that I never could have imagined.

I am proud of the choices I have made and the paths I have followed, yet I've always known I was being led down unfamiliar ones that I may not have chosen on my own. Be assured though, that they always, always turned out to be blessings. I always told Douglas that nothing is easy except for taking risks that get you into jail or lead to your death. Anything that is positive is only gotten through hard work, and if we didn't do it that way, we wouldn't appreciate our good fortune when it blessed us.

My life experiences and tragedy have groomed me for this moment. Ironically, my career has been a gradual build to where I am today. My career began working as the MOMs coordinator for the Pike County Extension Service, working with teen and at-risk mothers to decrease the county infant mortality rate. Second, I worked as the housing manager for the Troy Housing Authority, managing public housing and the Section 8 program. Then I was employed as a high school mathematics teacher and lastly, cementing my divine purpose, I worked as the housing manager for the United States embassy in Cairo, Egypt. Each of these jobs played a pivotal role in grooming me to where I am today and in allowing me to give back to my community. Today, I have testimonials from individuals from each of these milestone periods who have come to me and said, "I remember what you said to me," "You motivated me," "You were my mentor," "My college algebra was so easy because of you," or "I made it through basic training because of you, because I told myself if Mrs. Wilson did it, I can do it too."

I was determined not to end up a statistic, and I did not. My purpose now is to convey this message to as many others as I can while I am on this earth. Even though I have made a footprint in many lives and my prayer is to reach many more individuals, I know my message of resilience in the face of adversity, determination when all odds are against you, and perseverance when you feel you cannot go on can and will inspire, motivate, and uplift individuals facing the same experiences, tragedies, or who are simply needing a word of motivation.

I pray that this message will motivate you in some way, or help you to motivate someone else because in this life it's the light that someone sees in you that will make a difference in their life.

When life gives you only lemons, make lemonade...